THE CIVIL WAR

Photographs from the Special Collections
of the Library of Congress

A Book of Postcards

Pomegranate Artbooks, San Francisco

Pomegranate Artbooks
Box 6099
Rohnert Park, CA 94927

Pomegranate Europe Ltd.
Fullbridge House, Fullbridge
Maldon, Essex CM9 4LE
England

ISBN 1-56640-435-5
Pomegranate Catalog No. A629

Pomegranate publishes books of
postcards on a wide range of subjects.
Please write to the publisher for more information.

© Library of Congress
Designed by Allen Boyce Eddington
Printed in Korea

05 04 03 02 01 00 99   11 10 9 8 7 6 5

The resources of the Library of Congress are particularly rich and valuable in studying that unique and terrible event in American history, The Civil War. The Library's Manuscript Division has an unsurpassed collection of papers of the political and military leaders of the period, both Confederate and Union. The Geography and Map Division has a rich collection of printed and manuscript maps relating to the war. The vast majority were prepared by Federal forces or by commercial firms in the North, but there are also a substantial number by Confederate authorities, such as Jedediah Hotchkiss, mapmaker for General "Stonewall" Jackson.

The Music Division has an assemblage of Civil War sheet music numbering in the thousands. The Rare Book Division houses one of the largest groups of rare Confederate imprints and books relating to the Union; the distinguished collection of Lincolniana brought together by Alfred White Stern; and a large quantity of broadsides, including Union and Confederate recruiting posters, newspaper extras, and printed general orders.

Finally, there are the varied and comprehensive collections of the Prints and Photographs Division. Included are photographic negatives made by Mathew B. Brady and the staff of field photographers he organized to prepare a camera record of the war, original drawings by leading newspaper combat artists such as Edwin Forbes and Alfred R. Waud, and lithographic views of the war. The lithographic views range from inaccurate portrayals of battle action by Currier and Ives to the carefully reproduced "on-the-spot" sketches of soldier-artists. Foremost of these soldier-artists, as far as the Library's holdings are concerned, was Pvt. Alfred E. Matthews (31st Ohio); over thirty-five of his published drawings, among the finest of all Civil War lithographs, are in the collections.

THE CIVIL WAR

Col. E. E. Ellsworth

Ellsworth was the first Union officer to be killed by a
rebel after he removed the Confederate flag from the roof
of Marshall House in Alexandria, Virginia. He was shot by
proprietor Jim Jackson.

POMEGRANATE BOX 6099 ROHNERT PARK, CA 94927

THE CIVIL WAR

Gen. Robert E. Lee (seated), Gen. George W. C.
"Rooney" Lee (left) and Col. Walter Taylor (right)
This photograph was taken on the back porch of Lee's
Richmond home.

POMEGRANATE BOX 6099 ROHNERT PARK, CA 94927

THE CIVIL WAR

Union Ambulance Office, 9th Army Corps

POMEGRANATE   BOX 6099   ROHNERT PARK CA 94927

THE CIVIL WAR

Mathew Brady (wearing straw hat) and
Gen. Ambrose Burnside (reading newspaper)
This photograph was taken in early 1863 while Burnside was
in command of the Army of the Potomac, after his ill-fated
attack on Fredericksburg.

POMEGRANATE   BOX 6099   ROHNERT PARK, CA 94927

THE CIVIL WAR

Col. John S. Mosby and His Confederate Raiders

Mosby and his 43rd Virginia Cavalry were so successful
that a sizable portion of Virginia was known simply as
"Mosby's Confederacy."

POMEGRANATE   BOX 6099   ROHNERT PARK, CA 94927

THE CIVIL WAR

Abraham Lincoln (1809–1865)
Photograph by Mathew Brady, February 9, 1864

POMEGRANATE BOX 6099 ROHNERT PARK CA 94927

WANTED!

ONE HUNDRED AND ONE

Able-Bodied, Patriotic Men

TO FORM A COMPANY FOR THE

TENTH VERMONT REGIMENT.

Vermont has the honor of having sent out the first Regiment under the recent call for 300,000 Volunteers, and now a further requisition is made upon her loyalty and patriotism.

BRAVE MEN, FORWARD FOR THE TENTH !

THE FOLLOWING INDUCEMENTS ARE OFFERED FOR ENLISTING:

PAY AT THE RATE OF $20 PER MONTH.

$3,50 PER MONTH ALLOWED FOR CLOTHING.

$18 in advance, being one month's pay from the Government.

Twenty-Five Dollars Bounty in Advance,

And a further bounty of seventy-five dollars at the expiration of the term of enlistment.

THE COMPANY WILL RENDEZVOUS AND BE DRILLED

AT BRADFORD.

GEORGE P. BALDWIN,

Principal Recruiting Officer for Orange County.

Other Recruiting Offices at

THE CIVIL WAR

Vermont Recruiting Poster

POMEGRANATE BOX 6099 ROHNERT PARK, CA 94927

THE CIVIL WAR

Confederate Fort on Peachtree Street,
Atlanta, Georgia, looking south toward the city

POMEGRANATE BOX 6099 ROHNERT PARK CA 94927

THE CIVIL WAR

Gen. Ulysses S. Grant (1822–1885)

POMEGRANATE   BOX 6099   ROHNERT PARK, CA 94927

THE CIVIL WAR

Confederate Gun "Whistling Dick,"
Vicksburg, Mississippi

POMEGRANATE   BOX 6099   ROHNERT PARK, CA 94927

THE CIVIL WAR

Jefferson Davis (1808–1889)
Photograph by Mathew Brady & Co.

POMEGRANATE   BOX 6099   ROHNERT PARK, CA 94927

THE CIVIL WAR

Company E, 4th U. S. Colored Infantry, Fort Lincoln,
defenses of the city of Washington, c. 1863
Photograph by Mathew Brady

POMEGRANATE BOX 6099 ROHNERT PARK CA 94927

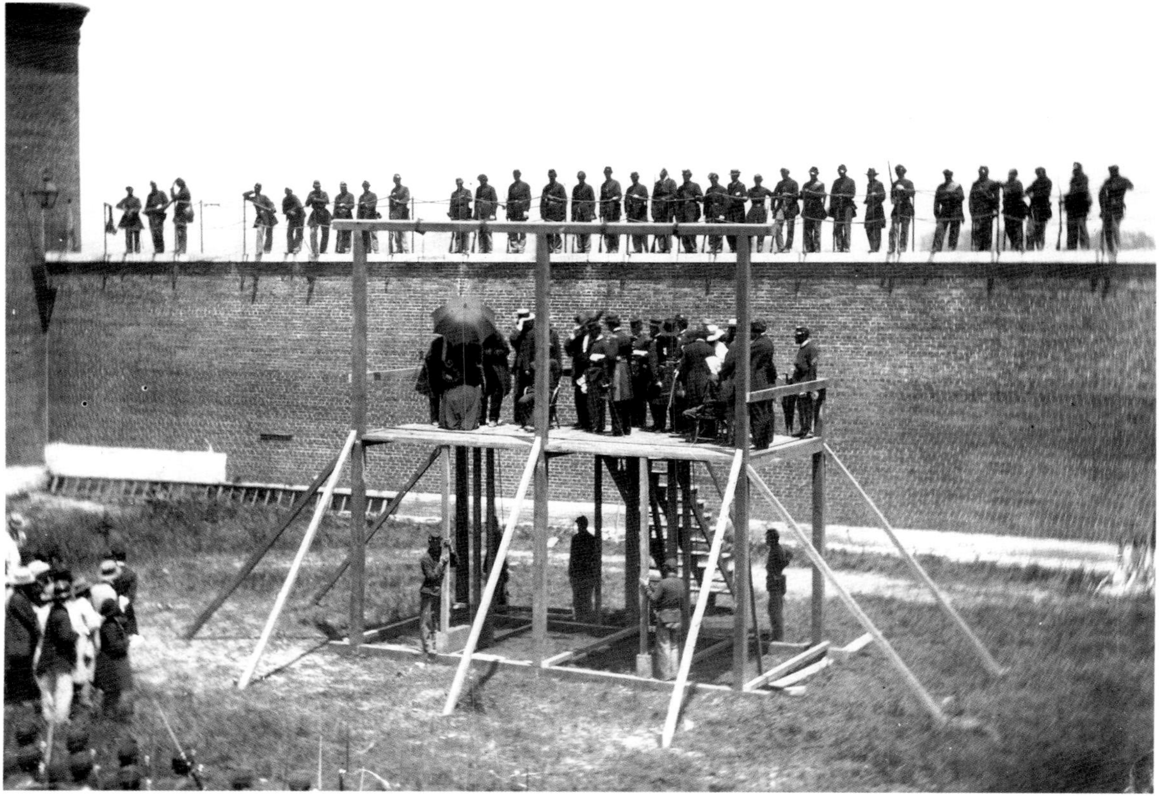

THE CIVIL WAR

The Lincoln Conspirators

The four condemned conspirators of the Lincoln assassination (Mrs. Surratt, Lewis Paine, David E. Herold, George A. Atzerodt) with officers and others on the scaffold, Washington, D. C., July 7, 1865

Photograph by Alexander Gardner

POMEGRANATE BOX 6099 ROHNERT PARK CA 94927

THE CIVIL WAR

Some of Gen. William Tecumseh Sherman's troops in abandoned Confederate trenches. To the right is the portable darkroom of photographer George N. Barnard.

POMEGRANATE BOX 6099 ROHNERT PARK CA 94927

THE CIVIL WAR

Gen. William Tecumseh Sherman and Staff

This photograph of Sherman (leaning on breach of gun)
and his staff was taken by George N. Barnard at Federal
Fort No. 7, Atlanta, Georgia, in 1864.

POMEGRANATE BOX 6099 ROHNERT PARK CA 94927

THE CIVIL WAR

Gen. Jubal Anderson Early, C.S.A. (1816–1894)
Photograph by Mathew Brady or Levin C. Handy

POMEGRANATE BOX 6099 ROHNERT PARK, CA 94927

THE CIVIL WAR

Mathew Brady's Photo Outfit

Brady set out to document the war with the belief it would last only a few months. In 1874 the War Department purchased Brady's negatives of the four-year conflict for the sum of $27,840.

POMEGRANATE   BOX 6099   ROHNERT PARK, CA 94927

THE CIVIL WAR

Men of the Ironclad *Monitor*

This photograph, taken in July 1862, shows the men who fought under the command of Lt. J. L. Worden during the contest with the *Virginia* (*Merrimac*). One of the nine famous dents in the turret is visible.

POMEGRANATE BOX 6099 ROHNERT PARK, CA 94927

THE CIVIL WAR

Lt. George Armstrong Custer (1839–1876)
The Peninsula, Virginia, 1862

In the Peninsular campaign of 1862, Custer distinguished himself as a brilliant cavalry officer. Brought to George McClellan's attention, he was promoted to captain of volunteers, only to be demoted to first lieutenant upon McClellan's retirement.

Pomegranate   Box 6099   Rohnert Park CA 94927

THE CIVIL WAR

Col. Micah Jenkins

Jenkins led the 5th South Carolina across Bull Run during the first battle there (July 1861), threatening McDowell's left flank and forcing a retreat. He was promoted to brigadier a year and a day later.

Pomegranate Box 6099 Rohnert Park CA 94927

THE CIVIL WAR

Maj. Gen. Joseph Wheeler, C.S.A.

Wounded three times during the war, "Fighting Joe"
Wheeler was considered by Robert E. Lee as one of his
two most brilliant cavalry officers. The other was Gen.
J.E.B. Stuart.

Pomegranate Box 6099 Rohnert Park CA 94927

THE CIVIL WAR

Ford's Theater, Washington, D.C., April 1865
Black crepe is draped across the facade of the theater
where Abraham Lincoln was assassinated.

Pomegranate Box 6099 Rohnert Park CA 94927

THE CIVIL WAR

The Mississippi River Fleet, Mound City, Illinois

POMEGRANATE BOX 6099 ROHNERT PARK CA 94927

THE CIVIL WAR

The Ruins of Montgomery Blair's House

Blair's house in Silver Spring was burned by Confederate soldiers under the command of Gen. Jubal Early. Montgomery Blair was postmaster-general of the United States.

POMEGRANATE BOX 6099 ROHNERT PARK CA 94927

THE CIVIL WAR

The Green Mountain Boys, 6th Vermont Co. I,
at Drill

POMEGRANATE BOX 6099 ROHNERT PARK CA 94927

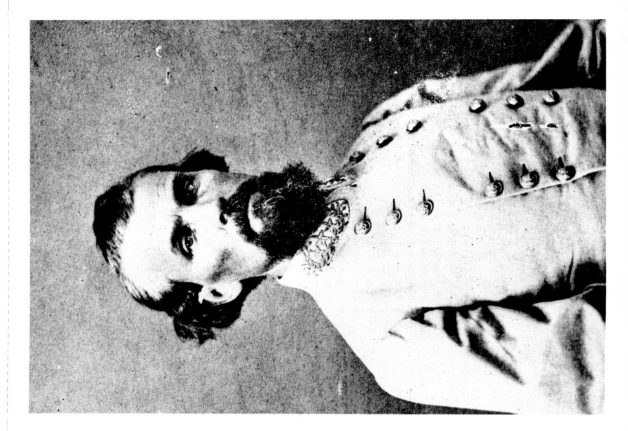

THE CIVIL WAR

Nathan Bedford Forrest, C.S.A. (1821–1877)

As a leader of mounted troops, Nathan Bedford Forrest had no equal. He was wounded several times, and it has been estimated that up to 29 horses were shot from under him.

POMEGRANATE   BOX 6099   ROHNERT PARK, CA 94927

Prints and Photographs Division, Library of Congress

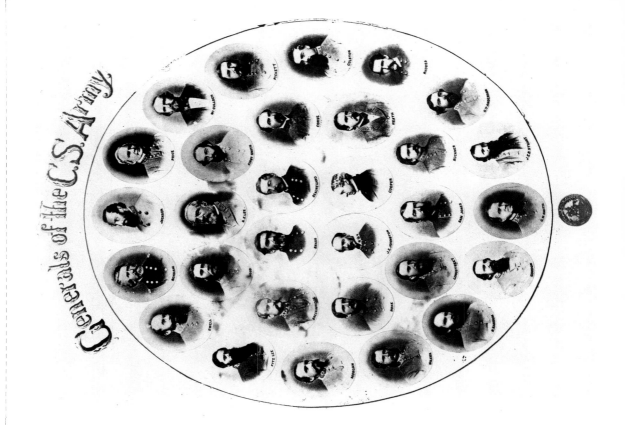

THE CIVIL WAR

Generals of the Confederate States Army

POMEGRANATE   BOX 6099   ROHNERT PARK CA 94927

THE CIVIL WAR

Gen. Albert Sidney Johnston, C.S.A.

Commander of the Confederate forces at Shiloh, Johnston
was killed during the battle. He was the highest-ranking
officer of either South or North to be killed in the war.

POMEGRANATE BOX 6099 ROHNERT PARK CA 94927

THE CIVIL WAR

USS *Galena*

This vessel was one of the first three Federal ironclads
tested in combat.

POMEGRANATE   BOX 6099   ROHNERT PARK CA 94927

THE CIVIL WAR

Headquarters, Army of the Potomac,
Petersburg, Virginia, August 1864
Shown here are captains Clinton, Kephardt, Coxe and
Stryher, and Lt. G. Lydisher of the U. S. Engineers.
One man is unidentified.

POMEGRANATE BOX 6099 ROHNERT PARK CA 94927